Rainer Strzolka

Soviet cult cameras. Traveling with the Lomo Sokol.

Images from Rethen

Berlin

Galerie für Kulturkommunikation

2019

Art or film waste?
Anyone traveling with a lomographic camera
can see better how colorful life can actually
be, if you do not look too closely.
Lomography is a phenomenon in its
absurdity of action. She can be addictive, she
can leave you cold. In any case, it is a piece
of freedom against the illusion of
digitalisation in photography that has turned
a camera into a computer that accidentally
takes pictures.
The examination of lomographic images
makes one dizzy.

And happy.

Rainer Strzolka

Rainer Strzolka (Berlin, Germany) makes photos and conceptual artworks. By studying sign processes, signification and communication, Strzolka makes work that generates diverse meanings. Associations and meanings collide. Space becomes time and language becomes image.

His photos are based on inspiring situations: visions that reflect a sensation of indisputability and serene contemplation, combined with subtle details of odd or eccentric, humoristic elements. With a subtle minimalistic approach, he wants the viewer to become part of the art as a kind of added component. Art is entertainment: to be able to touch the work, as well as to interact with the work is important.

His works question the conditions of appearance of an image in the context of contemporary visual culture in which images, representations and ideas normally function. By creating situations and breaking the passivity of the spectator, he creates work in which a fascination with the clarity of content and an uncompromising attitude towards conceptual and minimal art can be found. The work is aloof and systematic and a cool and neutral imagery is used.

His practice provides a useful set of allegorical tools for manoeuvring with a pseudo-minimalist approach in the world of photography: these meticulously planned works resound and resonate with images culled from the fantastical realm of imagination. Rainer Strzolka currently lives and works in Brela, Croatia.

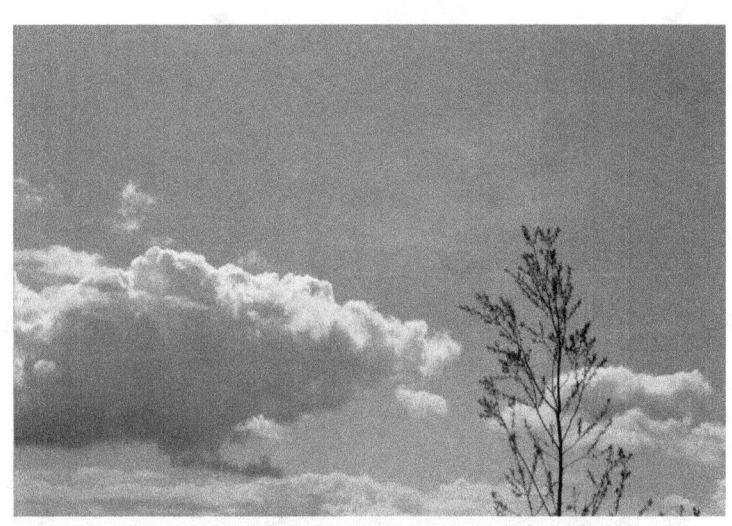

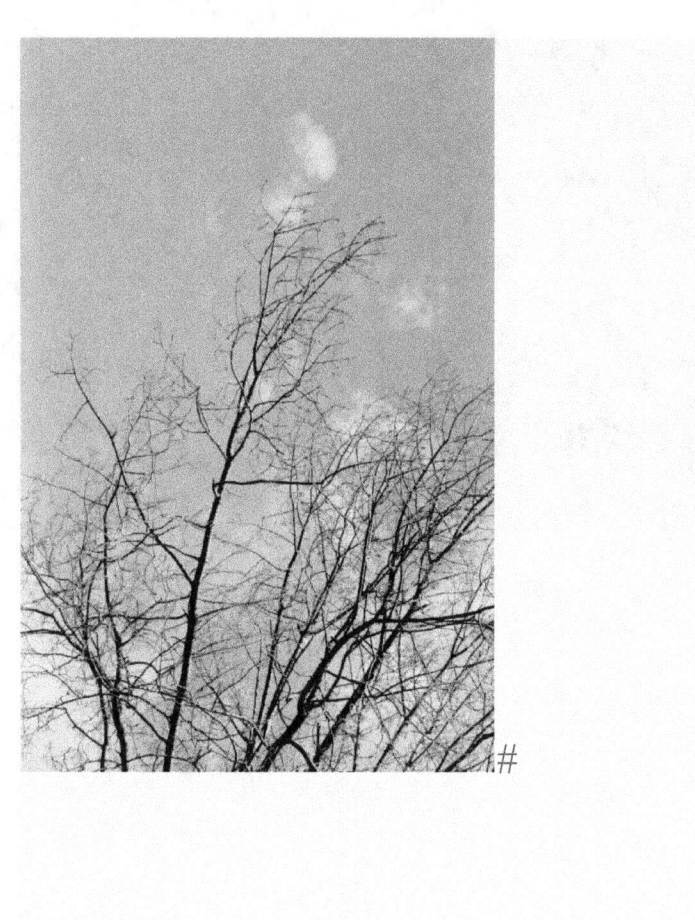

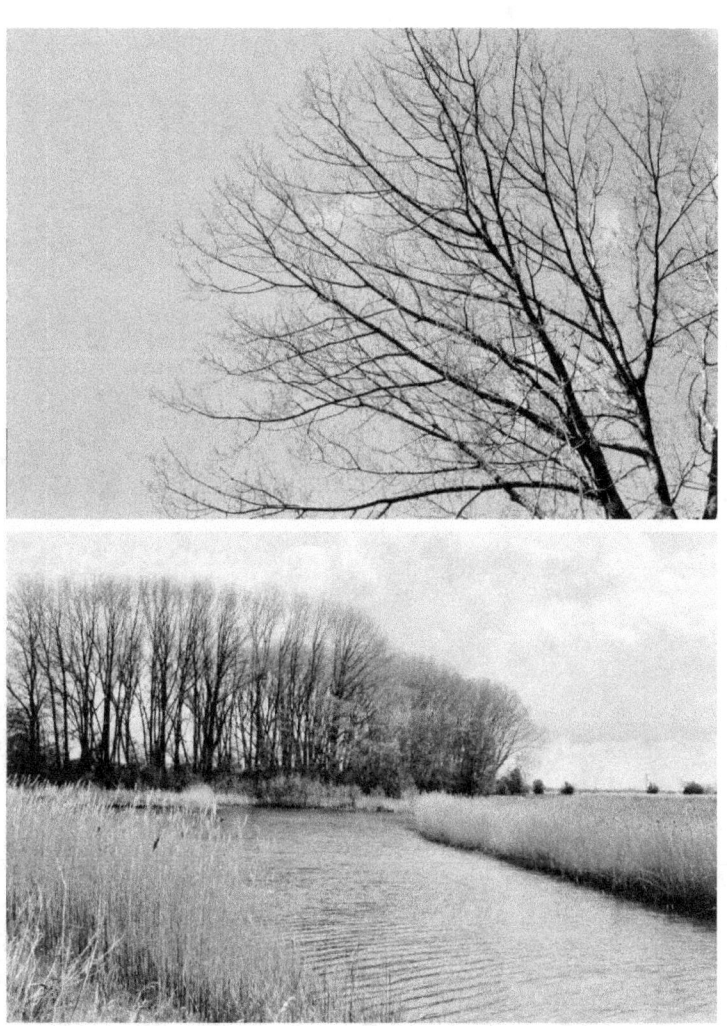

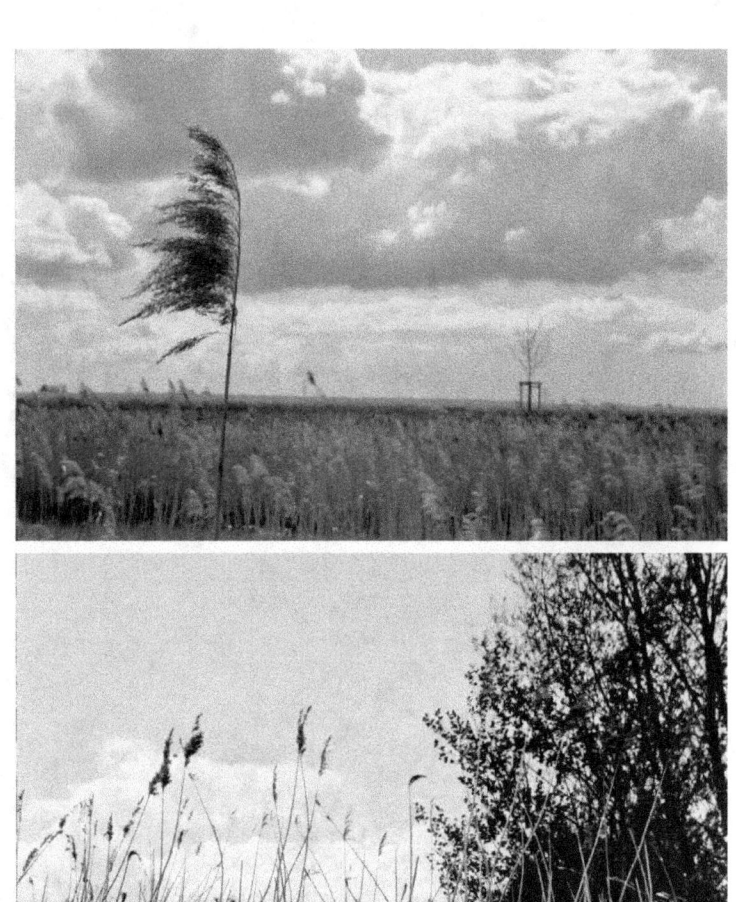

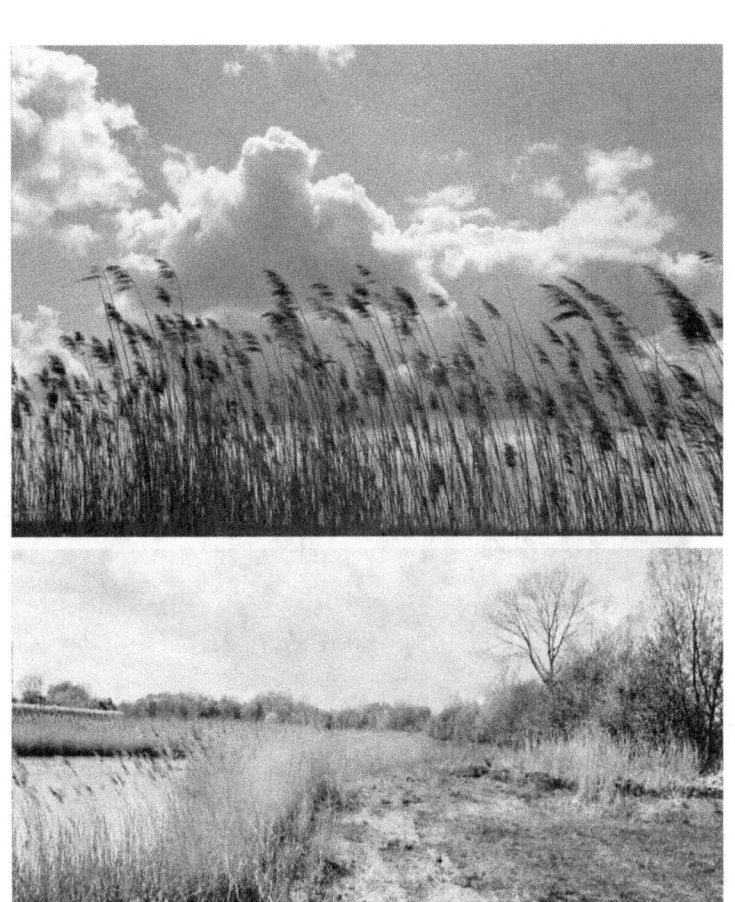

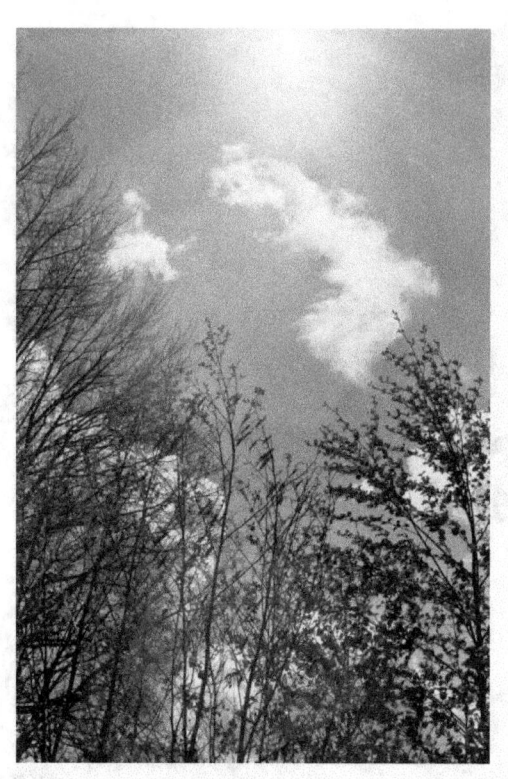

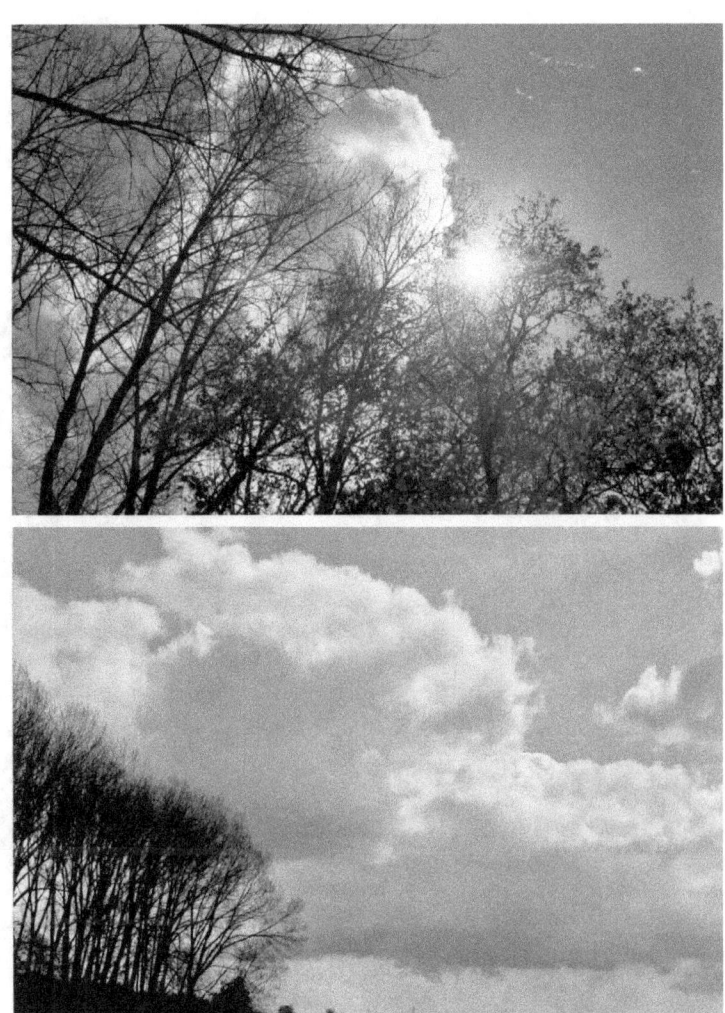

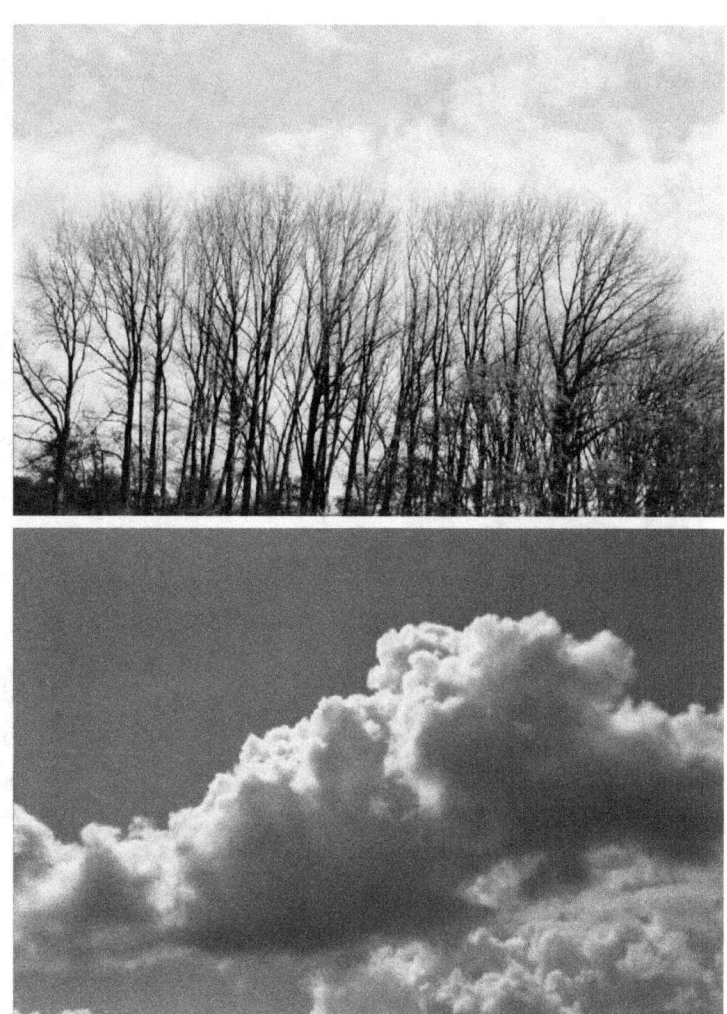

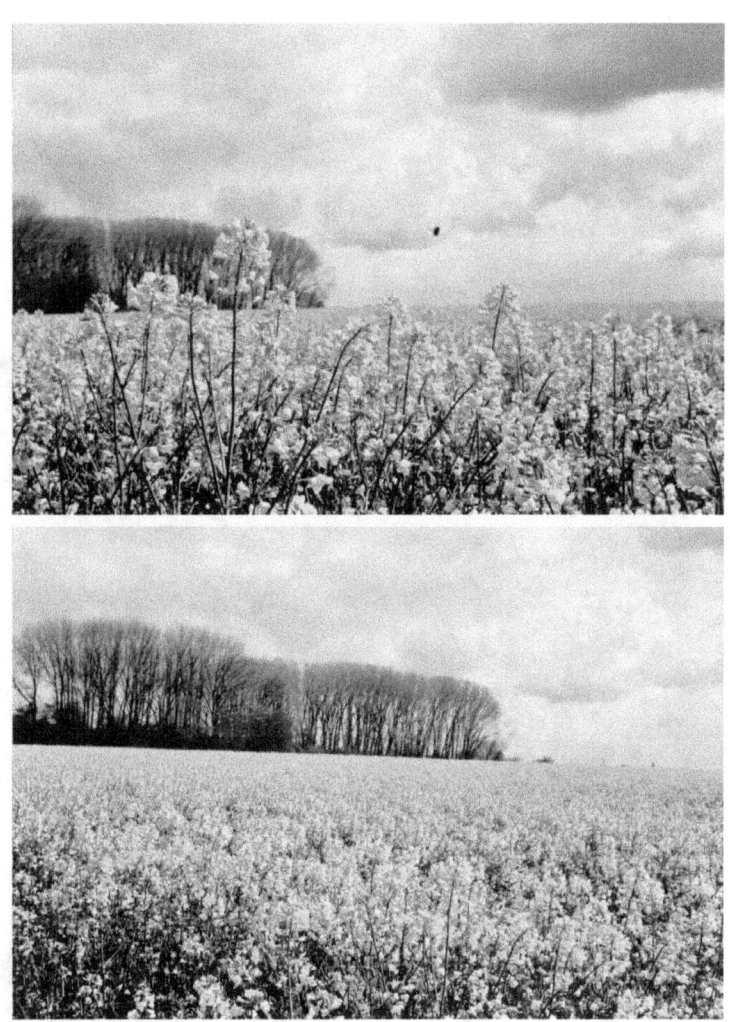

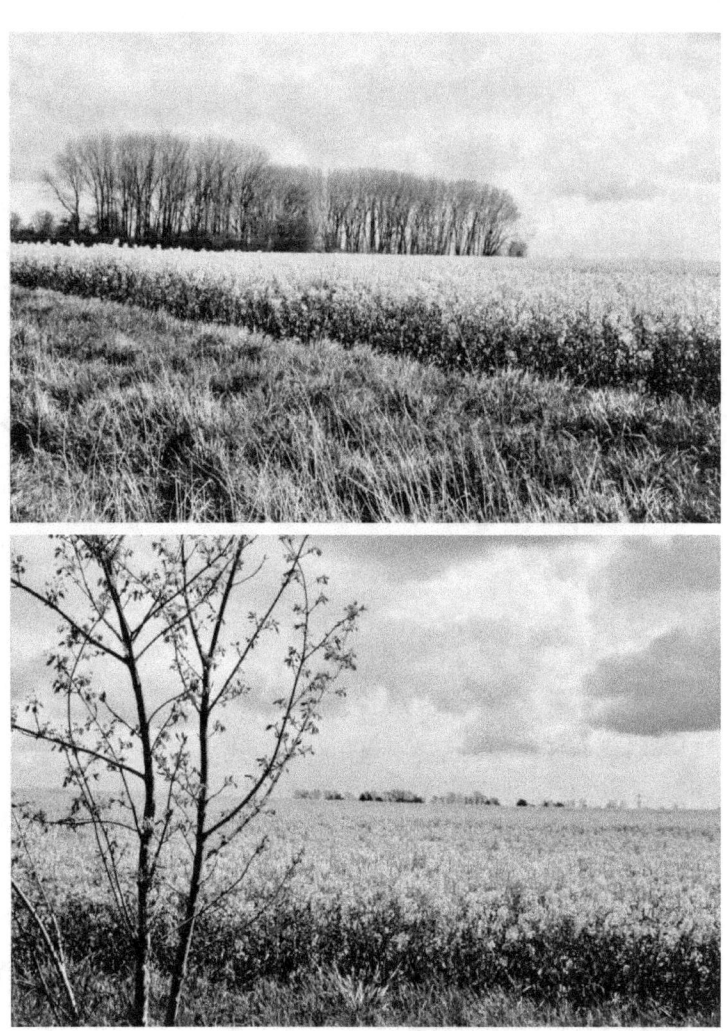

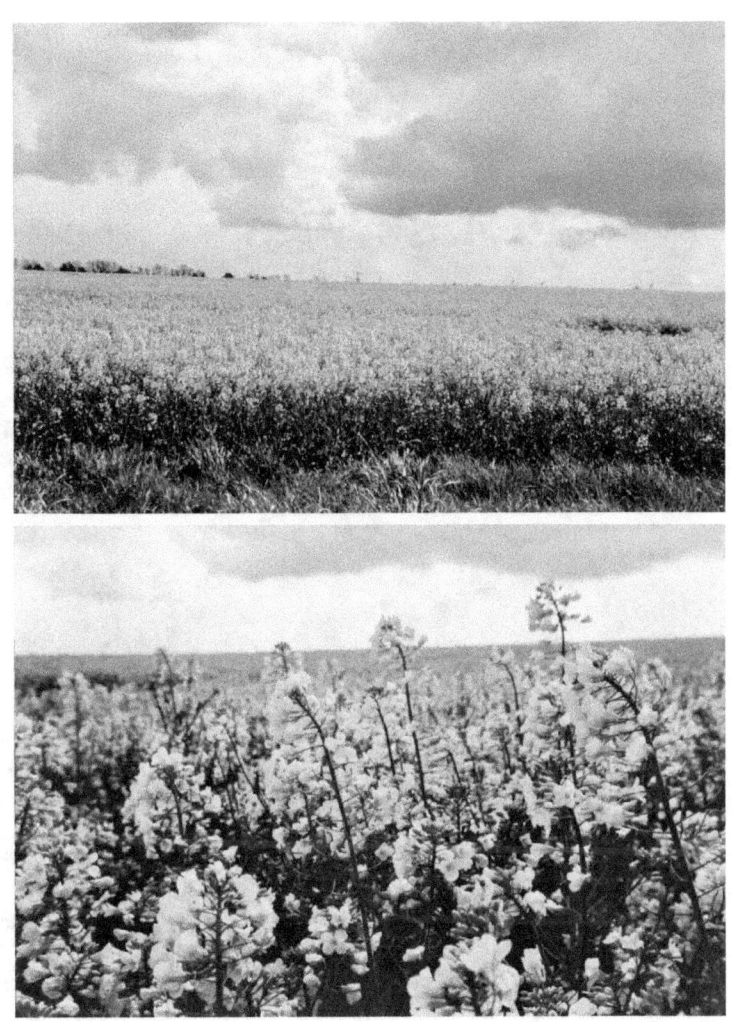

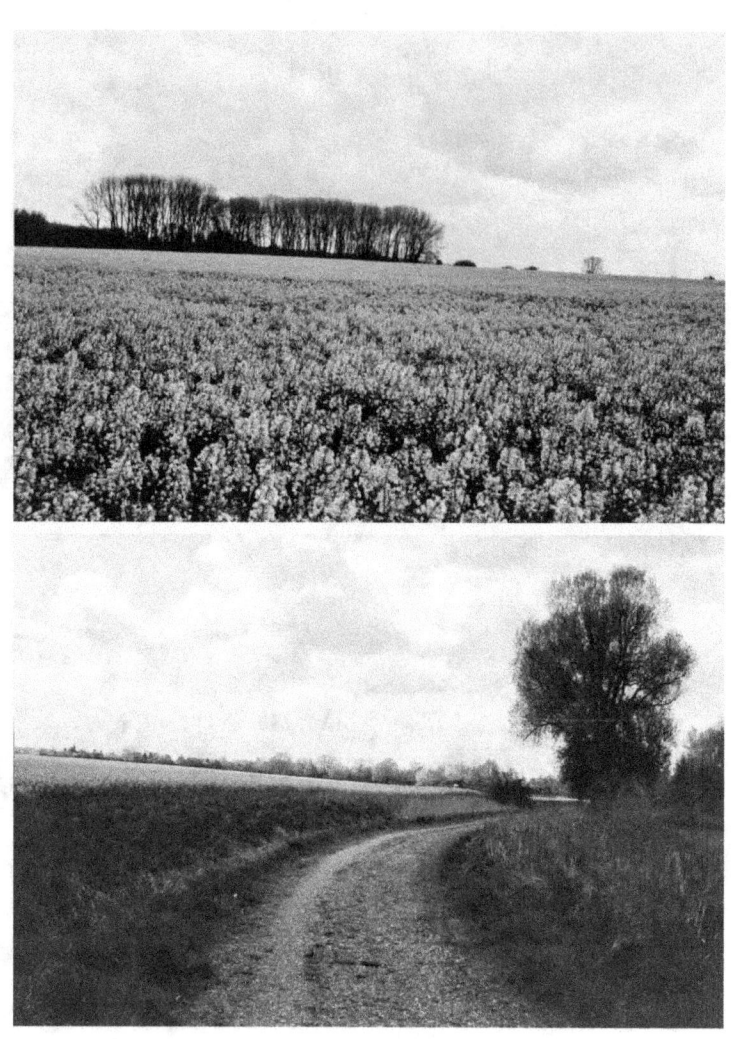

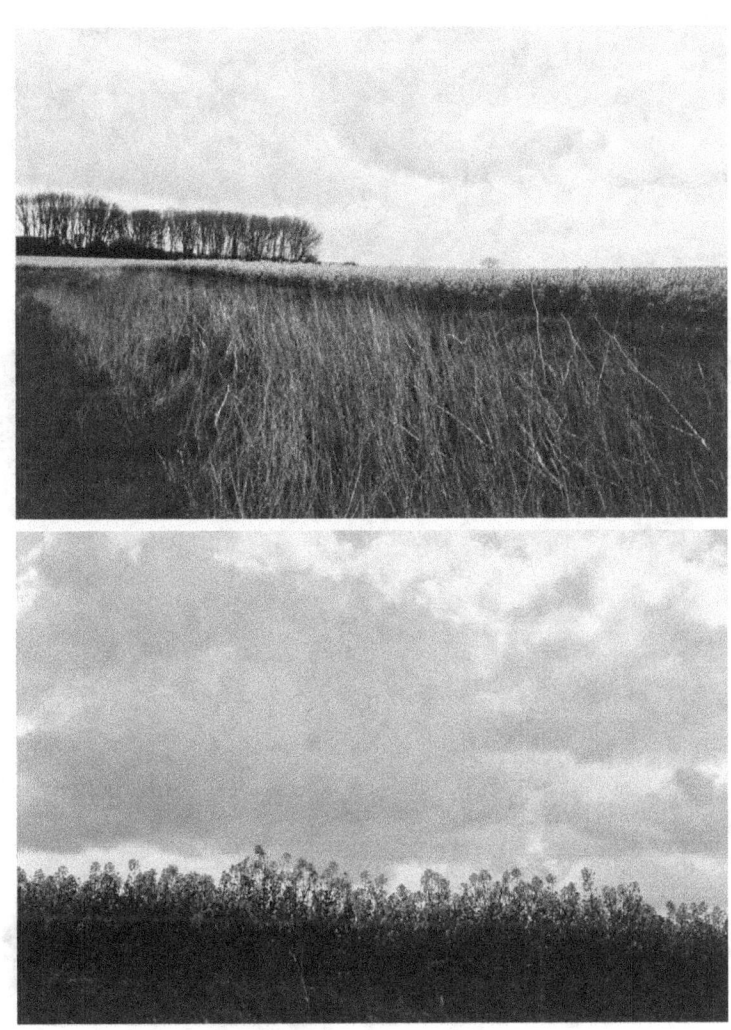

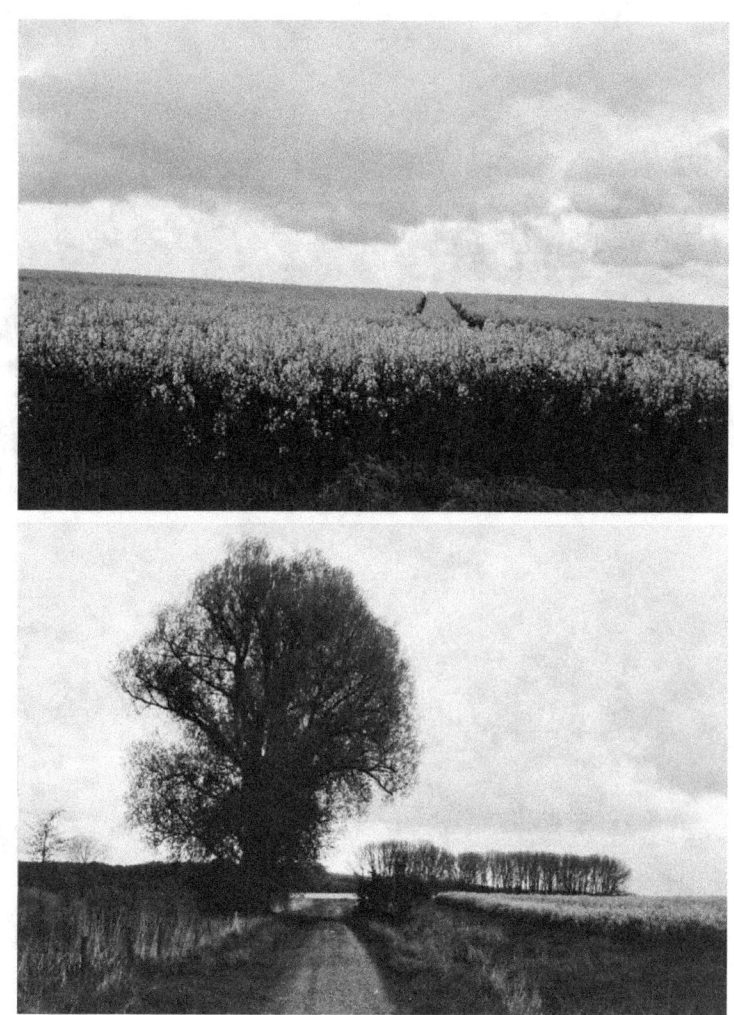

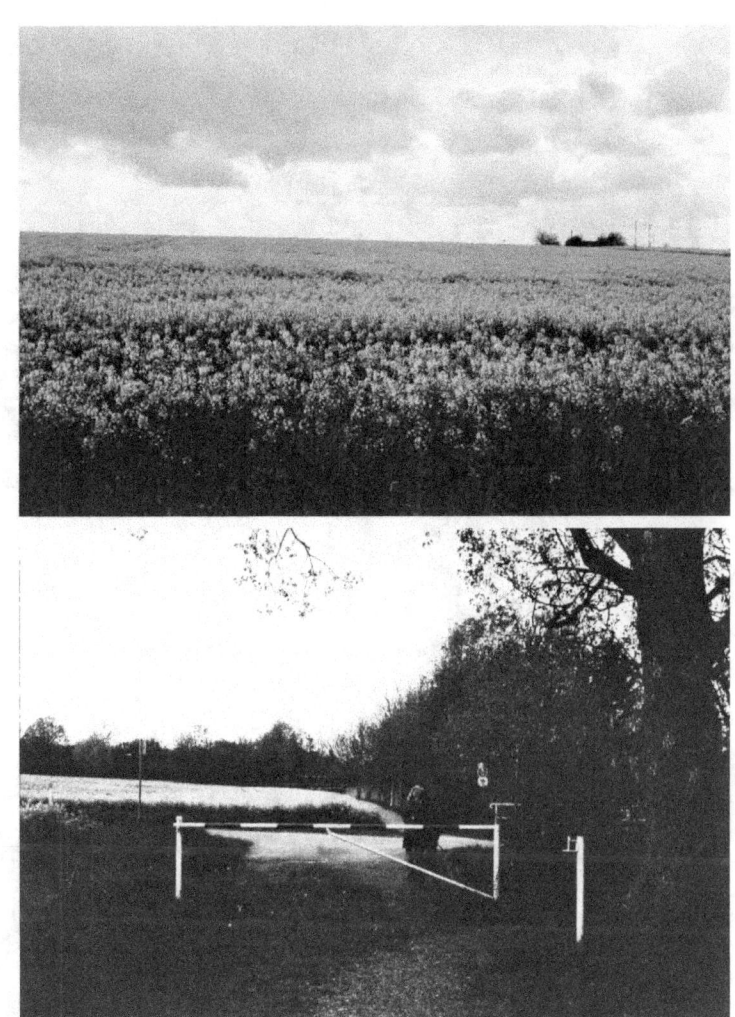

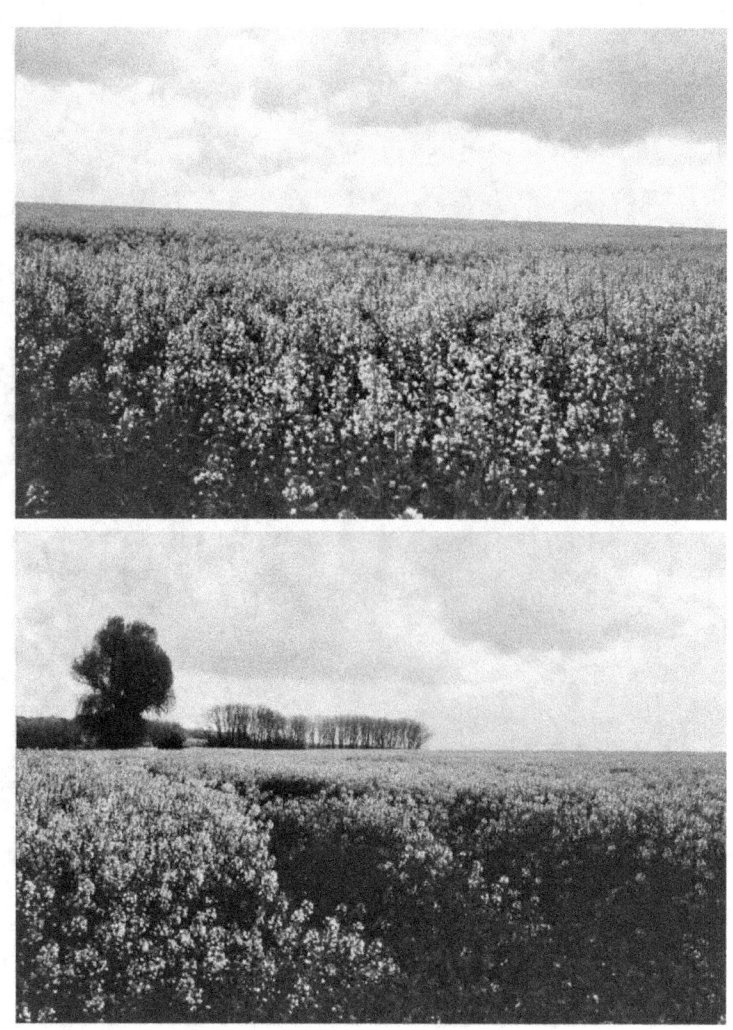

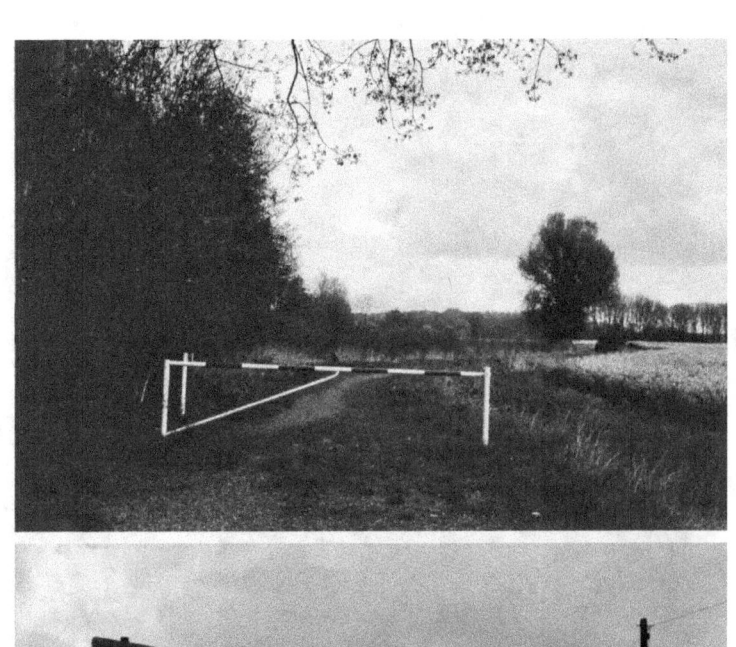
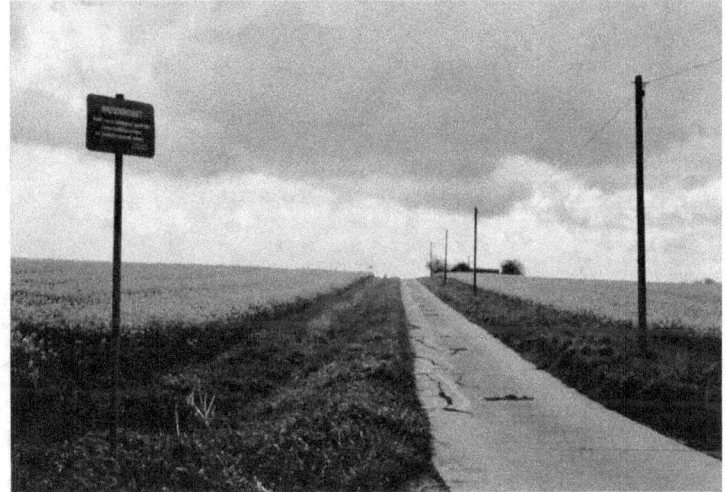

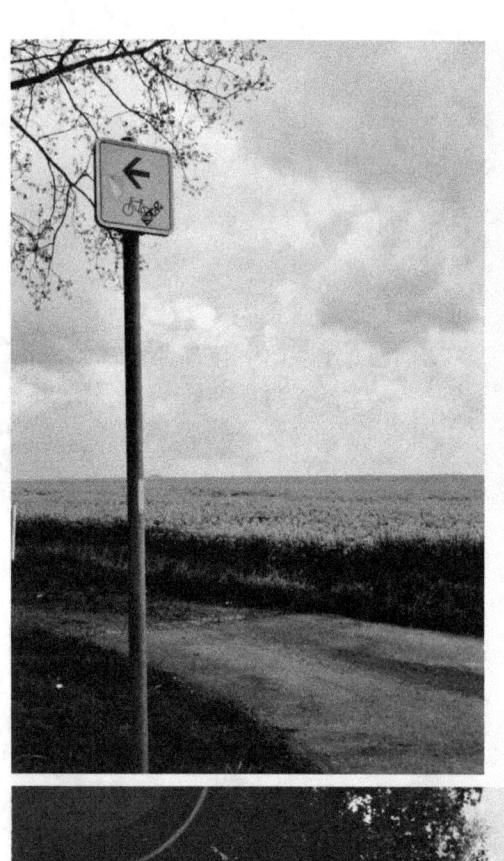

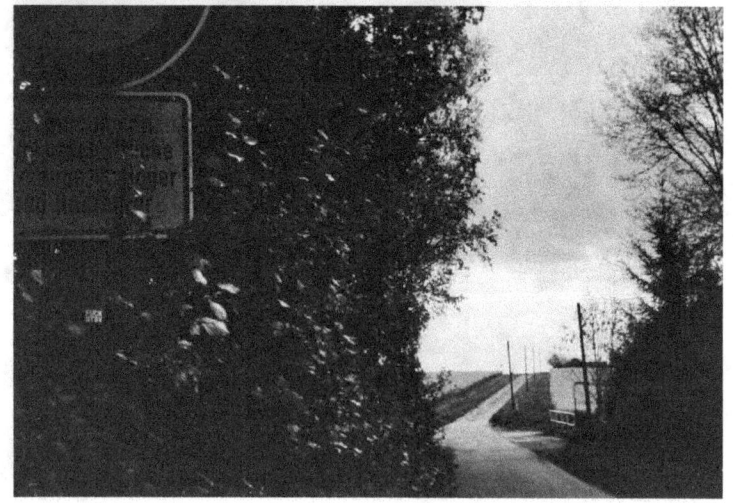

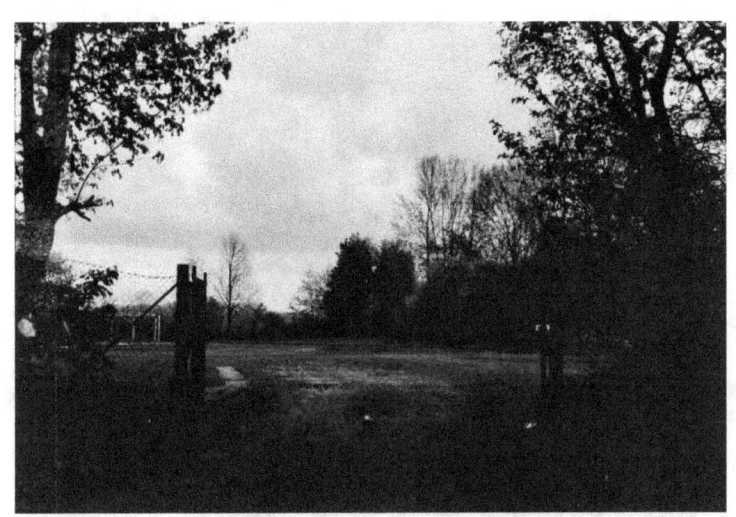

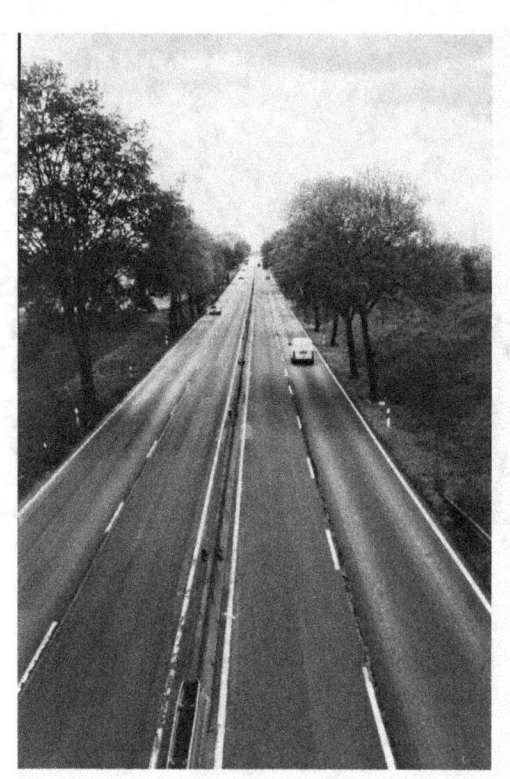

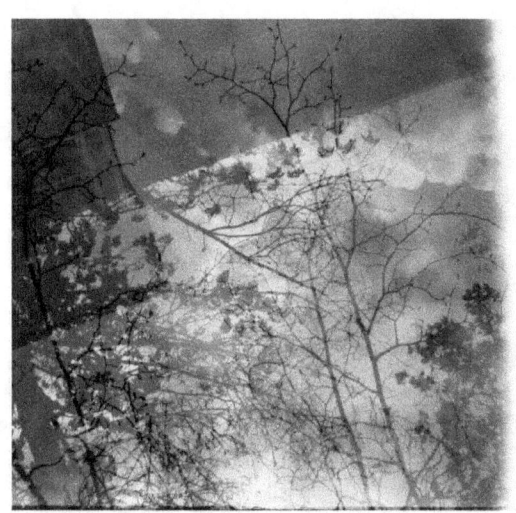